Girls Play
BASKETBALL

Amy B. Rogers

PowerKiDS
press™

New York

Published in 2017 by The Rosen Publishing Group, Inc.
29 East 21st Street, New York, NY 10010

First Edition

Editor: Katie Kawa
Book Design: Tanya Dellaccio

Photo Credits: Cover, p. 10 Debby Wong/Shutterstock.com; p. 4 https://commons.wikimedia.org/wiki/File:Naismith_statue,_Almonte.jpg; pp. 5, 22 Monkey Business Images/Shutterstock.com; p. 6 https://commons.wikimedia.org/wiki/File:Senda_Berenson.jpg; p. 7 (top) https://commons.wikimedia.org/wiki/File:Smith-College-Class-1902-basketball-team.jpg; p. 7 (bottom) https://commons.wikimedia.org/wiki/File:Official_Basketball_Guide_for_Women_(1915_edition).jpg; p. 8 William West/Getty Images; p. 9 DeCe/Shutterstock.com; p. 12 Rena Schild/Shutterstock.com; p. 13 Jeff Gross/Getty Images; p. 15 Jamie McDonald/Getty Images; p. 16 Photo Works/Shutterstock.com; p. 17 (top) Doug James/Shutterstock.com; p.17 (bottom) Nick Laham/Getty Images; p. 18 Hannah Foslien/Contributor/Getty Images; p. 19 (top) Jamie Sabau/Getty Images; p. 19 (bottom) Jeff Schear/Getty Images; p. 20 Kitra Cahana/Getty Images; p. 21 Joe Robbins/Getty Images.

Cataloging-in-Publication Data

Names: Rogers, Amy B.
Title: Girls play basketball / Amy B. Rogers.
Description: New York : PowerKids Press, 2017. | Series: Girls join the team | Includes index.
Identifiers: ISBN 9781499420937 (pbk.) | ISBN 9781499420951 (library bound) | ISBN 9781499420944 (6 pack)
Subjects: LCSH: Women's National Basketball Association–History–Juvenile literature. | Basketball for girls–Juvenile literature. | Basketball–History–Juvenile literature.
Classification: LCC GV886.R64 2017 | DDC 796–dc23

Manufactured in the United States of America

CPSIA Compliance Information: Batch #BS16PK For Further Information contact Rosen Publishing, New York, New York at 1-800-237-9932

CONTENTS

NOTHING BUT NET!

She shoots—she scores! Women have been playing basketball since the sport's earliest days more than a century ago. In 1891, James Naismith invented the sport of basketball in Springfield, Massachusetts. The next year, Senda Berenson Abbott created a version of Naismith's game to be played by the women she taught at Smith College in Northampton, Massachusetts.

Since that time, women's basketball has grown into a powerful force in the world of sports. The Women's National Basketball Association (WNBA) is the most successful **professional** sports **league** for women in the United States. Read on to learn more about how girls and women are leaving their mark on the basketball court!

Overtime!

Basketball got its name because Naismith had players throw the ball into peach baskets in order to score points.

Even the most famous WNBA players started out as young girls who loved to play basketball.

WOMEN'S BASKETBALL PIONEERS

Long before WNBA games were being played in **arenas** around America, the first women's basketball games were played in small colleges and other schools. It all started with Senda's gym classes at Smith College. Senda is sometimes called "the mother of women's basketball." She was the editor of the first official guide to playing basketball for women. She was also the chairperson, or leader, of the National Women's Basketball Committee for 12 years.

Another woman who helped the game of basketball grow in its early days was Clara Gregory Baer. In 1895, she **published** the first set of women's basketball rules.

Overtime!

Senda divided the court into three parts, and the players weren't allowed to leave their part of the court. In 1971, women were finally allowed to move over the whole court during a basketball game.

The first basketball game between two women's college teams took place on April 4, 1896, when Stanford University played the University of California, Berkeley. The earliest college basketball games looked very different from the games played today.

first official guide to women's basketball, edited by Senda Berenson Abbott

BASKETBALL BASICS

The rules of basketball have changed a lot since the time of Senda Berenson Abbott and Clara Gregory Baer. At first, the number of players on each team was anywhere from five to nine depending on factors such as the size of the court. Now, the game is always played between teams of five players.

When one of those five players scores, it's not always worth the same number of points. Most shots are worth two points. A shot made from beyond the three-point line is worth three points. A shot made from the free throw line after a **foul** is worth one point.

Overtime!

A dunk is a special kind of basketball shot that happens when a player jumps high enough to push the ball over the rim and through the basket. It's worth two points. On July 30, 2002, Lisa Leslie became the first WNBA player to successfully dunk during a game.

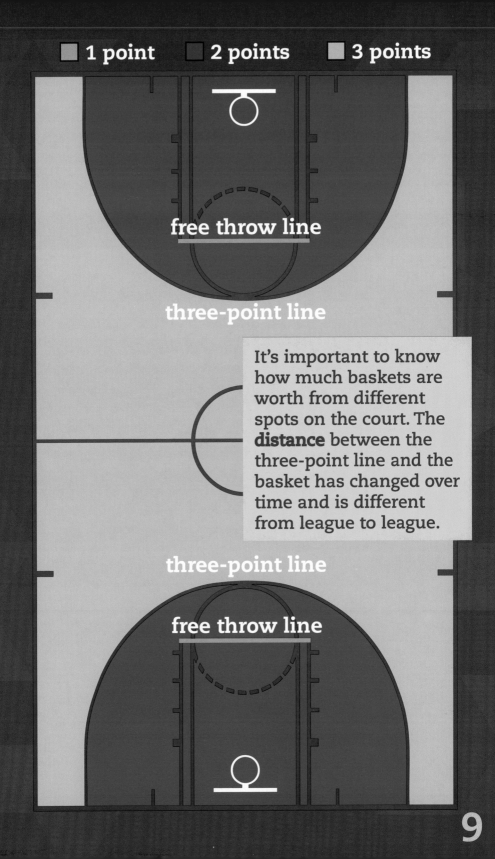

■ 1 point ■ 2 points ■ 3 points

free throw line

three-point line

It's important to know how much baskets are worth from different spots on the court. The **distance** between the three-point line and the basket has changed over time and is different from league to league.

three-point line

free throw line

PLAYING THE POSITIONS

In some sports, different players come into the game when their team is on offense (trying to score) or defense (trying to keep the other team from scoring). In basketball, the game moves so quickly that the five players on the court have to be good at both parts of the game.

There are three main positions on a basketball court: guard, forward, and center. A team generally has two guards, two forwards, and one center on the court during a game. Guards are sometimes separated into point guards and shooting guards, and forwards can be power forwards or small forwards.

Overtime!

Some basketball players can play more than one position. Elena Delle Donne, who was the 2015 WNBA Most Valuable Player (MVP), plays as both a guard and a forward.

shooting guard

★ takes shots and scores points

★ moves without the ball to get open for shots

center

★ often the tallest player on the team

★ gets **rebounds**

★ blocks other teams' shots

BASKETBALL POSITIONS

power forward

★ often plays close to the basket

★ helps the center by getting rebounds

small forward

★ makes plays from different parts of the court

★ plays well on offense and defense

point guard

★ often the smallest player on the team

★ has great ball-handling skills

★ sometimes called the "coach on the floor"

The rules only say there must be five players on the court. They don't say the specific positions they must play. This allows teams to get creative. For example, some teams play with three guards and no center.

GREAT COLLEGE TEAMS

If you want to be a basketball star, start playing as soon as possible. School teams are a great place to begin. If you work hard enough and have the right skills on the basketball court and in the classroom, you might be able to play this sport in college.

One of the most famous coaches in the history of college basketball is Pat Summitt. She led the University of Tennessee's women's basketball team to 1,098 wins before stepping down in 2012. As of 2016, no other college women's basketball coach has won more games.

Overtime!

In 1972, a law was passed requiring that schools that receive money from the **federal** government give girls and women the same opportunities to play sports as boys and men. This law, which is called Title IX or Title Nine, helped women's sports grow in a major way.

PAT SUMMITT

Another successful women's basketball team is found at the University of Connecticut. The Huskies have won 11 national **championships** as of 2016. Between 2008 and 2010, they won 90 straight games, which is a record for any college basketball program—men's or women's.

BASKETBALL AROUND THE WORLD

Playing basketball could take you all over the world! Although basketball started in the United States, it's now played around the globe. In fact, some American players have traveled to faraway countries to play basketball. Diana Taurasi, who was a star at the University of Connecticut and in the WNBA, traveled to Russia to play for a professional team there.

Every four years, the best basketball players in the world compete against each other at the Summer Olympics. Women's basketball became an Olympic sport in 1976. The United States has won more Olympic gold **medals** in women's basketball than any other country.

Overtime!

In 2012, the U.S. women's basketball team won its fifth straight Olympic gold medal. That's a record number of gold medals in a row for a **traditional** women's team sport at the Olympics.

Being in a wheelchair doesn't have to stop you from being a superstar basketball player! The best wheelchair basketball players in the world compete against each other during the Paralympic Games.

THE WNBA

In school gyms and on playground courts, girls play basketball with their friends and pretend they're playing for a WNBA championship. That wasn't always a dream for girls who loved to play basketball—the WNBA isn't that old! It started in 1997 after several other professional leagues for women tried and failed to find lasting success.

The WNBA started with eight teams. As of 2016, it has 12 teams. Past WNBA stars—including Lisa Leslie, Tina Thompson, and Sheryl Swoopes—helped the league grow. Current WNBA stars serve as role models for girls on and off the court.

Overtime!

As of 2015, Tina Thompson holds the record for most points scored by a WNBA player. She scored 7,488 points during her time in the league!

WNBA players prove that "playing like a girl" means playing with toughness, talent, and teamwork.

Sheryl Swoopes

WNBA ROLE MODELS

Maya Moore is one of the WNBA's brightest stars. She showed what hard work and talent can do even before she reached the WNBA. She was the captain of the University of Connecticut team that won 90 straight games. Maya then began playing for the WNBA's Minnesota Lynx. As of 2015, she's won three WNBA championships.

Skylar Diggins is a WNBA All-Star who's making a difference off the court, too. She started Skylar's Scholars to recognize kids who've overcome challenges to **achieve** great things in the classroom. Skylar also speaks out about how important it is for kids to stay active.

Overtime!

Maya Moore won an Olympic gold medal in 2012.

Skylar Diggins

Maya and Skylar host basketball camps. They teach kids skills they can use to become better basketball players and leaders on and off the court. Many other WNBA players also host basketball camps around the country.

COOL CAREERS

If you like playing basketball but don't dream of becoming a WNBA star, there are still plenty of cool **careers** you can choose. If you enjoy being a leader and coming up with basketball plays, you could be a coach. Women coach in the WNBA, in college, and even in the National Basketball Association (NBA)—the highest American professional league for men. Becky Hammon is an assistant coach for the NBA's San Antonio Spurs. She was the first woman to become a full-time NBA assistant coach.

If you like talking about basketball, you could become a commentator, or a person who talks about the game on television or the radio. Doris Burke and Kara Lawson are two current female basketball commentators.

Overtime!

In 2015, Becky Hammon became the first woman to coach an NBA summer league team. Her team won the summer league championship that year!

Girls who play basketball learn important skills that can help them in their future careers. The women shown here are great at their jobs because they learned so much about basketball while playing it.

Doris Burke

STAYING FIT AND MAKING FRIENDS

Basketball has been helping girls stay fit and make friends for more than 100 years. Girls who play basketball learn much more than just how to shoot a ball or play good defense. They learn the value of teamwork, practice, and doing their best. These lessons are taught everywhere from small-town playgrounds to college courts and WNBA arenas.

Girls who play basketball are given tools to help them grow into strong women. Does this sport sound like fun? Grab a ball, find a basket, and give it a try. You might have what it takes to make it in the WNBA!

GLOSSARY

achieve: To get by effort.

arena: An enclosed area used for public entertainment.

career: A job a person can do for a long time.

championship: A contest to find out who's the best player or team in a sport.

distance: The space between two points.

federal: Relating to the central government of the United States.

foul: An act that breaks the rules in a game or sport.

league: A group of teams that play the same sport and compete against each other.

medal: A flat, small piece of metal with art or words that's used as an honor or reward.

professional: Having to do with a job someone does for a living.

publish: To print a written work and present it to the public.

rebound: The act of catching the basketball after a shot has missed going in the basket.

traditional: Following what's been done for a

INDEX

WEBSITES

Due to the changing nature of Internet links, PowerKids Press has developed an online list of websites related to the subject of this book. This site is updated regularly. Please use this link to access the list:
www.powerkidslinks.com/gjt/bball